# Berries, Rasp- & Black

by Louise Riotte

## Blueberry Plants

Need consistent watering (moist)
use netting for protection
Mulch
prune while dormant (older stems)
fertilize in spring before
leaves have grown in
(once a year)

# Raspberries in the Home Garden

The brambles, raspberries and blackberries, are among the most popular of all bush fruits, ranking second for most families only to the strawberry. I have found them easy to grow and very rewarding, for they produce the most fruit with the least amount of effort. Blackberries will be considered separately, so let's start with the raspberries.

Raspberries bear a light crop the second year after planting but you can expect a full crop a year later, and annual crops thereafter for the life of the planting. And plantings that are well cared for may produce good crops for ten years or more.

Another big advantage I've found with raspberries is the relative ease of controlling insects and diseases as compared with the sometimes difficult, expensive and messy job of applying several sprays each year to fruit trees. The berries often need **no** spraying, but if they do, it may be done with a hand sprayer or duster.

While generally raspberries thrive best in cooler regions, I have had no difficulty growing them in my area of southern Oklahoma, and have been particularly successful with the black ones, such as the **Cumberland** variety. The red variety, **Latham**, has done well for me, too, but may be expected to do much better farther north.

Raspberries come in a brilliant spectrum of colors — red, black, purple and yellow — and many varieties come early, midseason, late or as everbearers. Those bearing one large crop each year generally are referred to as "July-bearers."

The so-called "everbearers" are becoming increasingly popular, since they bear two crops each year and extend the season. If you have the space, plant both types.

Red raspberries include **Fallred** (everbearer), **Latham** (late), **Newburgh** (midseason), **September** (everbearer), **Southland** (everbearer), **Sunrise** (early) and **Taylor** (late). Some excellent varieties for the North, originated at the New York Experiment Station at Geneva, are **New Heritage**, a vigorous grower of medium-sized, very firm berries, which may be picked about September 1st. The sturdy, erect canes require no support. Two other excellent new varieties, **Hilton** and **Milton**, will be available soon as virus-free stocks can be increased.

Some good, proven varieties of black raspberries are **Allen** (early), **Black-hawk** (late), **Bristol** (midseason), **Cumberland** (midseason), **Dundee** (midseason), **New Logan** (early) and **Morrison** (late). Two fine varieties originated at the New York Station are **Huron**, which has large and glossy black berries of good quality, and **Jewel**, a vigorous variety whose large, glossy black fruits are of very high quality. The plant is not susceptible to any serious disease and only slightly susceptible to mildew.

The "purple" raspberry is a cross between reds and blacks. Varieties include **Amethyst** (midseason), **Clyde** (late) and **Purple Autumn** (an everbearer). **Sodus**, also an old favorite among the purples, is hard to beat.

Yellow raspberries include **Amber** (very late), **Fallgold** ( an everbearer) and **Forever Amber** (a yellow member of the black raspberry family). This last has medium-sized yellow-to-amber berries, which have a delicate black raspberry flavor and aroma.

Names of raspberry varieties seem almost endless when you look through nursery catalogs and it is difficult not to become confused. Each one, seemingly, has its own good qualities and differs from the others in size, quality, color or bearing season. It may be well for you to do a little detective work before you purchase. Check with your county agent, friends and neighbors, to find out what will grow best in your area and select types best adapted to your section of the country. One-year-old No. 1 grade plants are best for establishing new plantings. Make every effort to secure virus-free plants.

## Locating Your Raspberry Patch

Never try to grow raspberries in soil that is too acid—a pH of 6.0 is preferable—and determine your conditions by sending a soil sample to your State Agricultural College or Experiment Station. If you do not know where to send your sample, call your county agent.

To take a soil sample, dig deeply in four or five places in your plot, mix the earth together in a clean box and then send about a pint of this mixture. There probably will be a small charge for the test.

If the report shows an acidity below pH 5.8 or 6.0 you will need to give your plot a good application of lime. A one hundred foot row should have about 40 pounds of agricultural lime scattered on the ground, preferably in the fall before setting out plants in the spring. The lime should be dug or tilled into the ground, and if this is done in the fall, follow up by seeding the ground with rye.

If you're planning a hedge or single row of raspberries, lime, till and seed to rye a strip six or eight feet wide. You will need about six quarts of rye seed, which should be raked or cultivated into the ground.

In selecting your raspberry plot, bear in mind that the planting will remain there for seven to 10 years, so put it to one side of your garden where it will not interfere with yearly cultivation. Try to choose a piece of ground that has goodly amount of humus in it. If the soil is lacking, work into it a *very heavy application* of farmyard manure before sowing the rye. Manure with a lot of straw in it is excellent. If manure or compost is not available, gather grass clippings, weeds, wild grass or old vegetable plants from the garden. Till these into the ground with 50 pounds of purchased dried sheep manure. Do not use dried weeds with mature seed heads (as the seeds may sprout), but young, green weeds will decompose quickly.

Old leaf mold from a nearby woods can be used, but be sure to add lime even if the soil test shows alkaline or neutral, for leaf mold is acid, and the lime will be needed to counteract the condition. Old, weathered hay which is no longer fit for animal consumption, also may be used, or alfalfa and peanut hay, which are particularly high in nitrogen.

## Spring Care

In the spring, as soon as the soil can be worked, dig or plow in the rye. Do not use any fertilizer at this time. Then let the ground remain in the rough until you are ready to set out your raspberry plants. (This should be done about the time beans are planted in the garden in your section of the country.)

If you buy your plants from a reliable nurseryman you should order them in January or early February at the latest; let him decide when to send them to you. As soon as they arrive will be the right time to set them out in your locality. Unless you live in the far South or Southwest, spring is best to set out plants.

When the plants arrive, remove them from their packing at once (unless they are frozen—in which case let them thaw slowly in a cold room), and soak them in a tub of water to which enough soil has been added to make the water muddy. Muddy water not only freshens up the plants, but the particles of mud stick to the fine, hairlike roots. This helps the plants get a good start when they are set out.

## Fall Planting

I believe there is much to be said for fall planting if you live in a section of the country, as I do, where winters are **not too severe.** Raspberries set out during the autumn months will start growth early the following spring—just as soon as weather conditions are favorable and usually before it is feasible to do any spring planting. Thus, fruits planted in the fall get off to a quicker start and are apt to make better growth than spring-planted fruits. This advantage is particularly evident during the first season of growth.

Soil frequently is in better condition for planting, also, during the fall than in the spring, when sometimes it is so wet that planting must be delayed to prevent puddling or serious compaction. Raspberries should **never** be planted if the soil is excessively wet. Store the plants in a cool place and wait until things dry out. Then your soil will not pack.

Avoiding compaction is very important, because of the **leader buds.** When your raspberries arrive from the nursery you will note several small, pale colored, yellow-green growths on the stems just above the roots. Once the plant is set in the ground the buds soon will push their way upward and become little shoots, but packed soil will slow them down or make it impossible for them to come through.

In raspberry language these shoots are called canes. And they must have all the help you can give them, for they need to hurry and grow very fast. Their life lasts for only a little more than a year. You can see what an advantage it is, then, to plant in the fall if possible, so these little shoots can come through and grow quickly.

Another possible advantage of fall planting is the fact that nursery plants are generally fresher at this time than in the spring. Most frequently (but not always) nurseries dig their plants in autumn and store them bare-rooted during the winter. In this way, plants are available for early shipment the next spring. Although winter storage is not particularly detrimental, transplanting operations cause less of a setback when plants are replanted soon after they are dug.

Fall planting is best done in late October or early November, before the soil is frozen. The greatest drawback to it is possible heaving and winter-killing. Heaving of plants during the winter is caused by alternate freezing and thawing of the soil, and usually occurs when there is a lack of protecting snow. You can achieve equal or better protection by mulching your fall-planted bushes to a depth of six or eight inches with straw, hay, grass clippings or some similar material.

6

In extremely cold climates you can avoid winterkilling by mounding soil about a foot deep around your plant and over the roots. This mound should be removed in the spring.

## Hill or Hedge System?

If you intend to make a hedge row of your berry patch, set the plants about three feet apart in the row. If you want more than one row, be sure that they are not closer than five feet apart. If, on the other hand, you choose to set the plants in the hill system, the plants should not be set nearer than four or five feet apart each way. As the plants attain their full growth, the individual hills should be staked and the plants tied to each stake with heavy binding twine.

The hill system has the advantage of allowing free air circulation around individual plant clusters. When the hedge row system is used, often the rows are allowed to grow too thick and too wide. This causes berry mold and a chance for plant disease due to inadequate air circulation and lack of sun. If enough space is available, I feel the family wanting six to a dozen plants to supply its own needs will find the hill system the best to use.

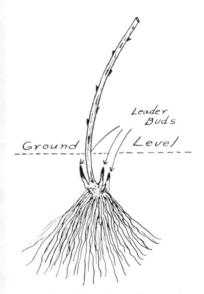

Newly planted raspberry plant showing position of leader buds placed on stem just above roots. Leave soil loose at surface of ground so buds can emerge. Set Red Raspberries 2 to 3 inches deeper than they were in the nursery, set Black and Purple about one inch deeper.

## How To Plant

Set your plants in holes large enough to contain the roots without crowding. Set red raspberries two to three inches deeper than they were in the nursery, and set black and purple raspberries about one inch deeper. Yellow raspberries, considered to be members of the black raspberry group, are also set about an inch deeper. You can determine this nursery depth by the dark brown color line on the cane.

Be sure to press dirt firmly about the plant roots. Do this by stepping around the plant, watering well to prevent air pockets. If the weather is dry put on a light mulch.

Red raspberry plants should be cut back to eight to 12 inches after planting. The canes, or the "handles" of black and purple raspberries should be cut off at ground level, removed from the planting and burned.

If there are any wild brambles growing around or near your new planting, they should be dug up and destroyed to prevent the possibility of their carrying disease.

7

# Cultivation

During the first season, cultivate the raspberry plants each week. Take care not to cultivate too deeply (as this may injure the feeder roots) and do not get too close to the plants. Continue cultivation until about August first but not after this, since it is important for the new canes to "harden off" in preparation for the winter. Cultivation after August first could stimulate new growth which in colder climates will winter-kill.

At this time you may cut off the original plant canes which you set out, as they will not bear again. The fruit will appear next year on this year's new canes.

If you have let weeds grow, cut them down before they go to seed and use them with all the other plant material you can find for mulch. It is good to place a layer of leaves four to six inches deep around the plants. Any kind will do, but if they are maple leaves do not use quite as many, as they have a tendency to pack. Oak leaves are the best, but they should be sprinkled with a little lime since they are very acid. If you use the mulch system—which I find very satisfactory—you will have nothing to do after August first other than put the mulch on about mid-October.

*Mulches not only conserve moisture as well as add organic matter, but also keep infecting organisms in the soil from splashing up on the plants during rains.*

*Things to remember:*
1. *Mulch should be applied following a light rain or after irrigation.*
2. *If mulch is too deep the benefit from a light rain will be lost.*
3. *Do not mulch wet-natured or poorly drained soils.*
4. *Decomposing materials will use up moisture.*
5. *Mulch is especially beneficial in the summer to conserve moisture. In the winter it will help to prevent heaving.*
6. *Never burn off a mulch. Either remove it for future use, or turn it into the soil.*
7. *If hay or straw is used, pre-sprout any harmful weed, grass or grain seed that may be present by sprinkling or soaking the material with water for two or three weeks prior to use.*

If you prefer to cultivate instead of mulching, stop cultivation by August first and in mid-September rake into the ground a heavy sowing of rye. Take care not to get the rye too close to the plants or it will be difficult to remove the following spring.

Use leaves close to the plants, let the rye grow over the fall and winter, and in early spring dig or till it into the ground. Again, do not till or cultivate too deeply near the plants. When you work the rye into the ground it is good to add some well-decomposed compost, too.

If you use the mulch system, till the mulch into the soil in the early spring, also adding a light application of compost or well-decayed manure. This should be done early, whether it is rye or another mulch. If you wait too long, you will break off the new raspberry canes which will have started into growth. Again place more mulch on the raspberry patch—weeds, straw, leaves—anything organic that is available.

## Pruning

Understanding how raspberries grow and bear fruit helps us to understand why they should be trained and pruned by certain methods. They bear their fruit on **biennial** canes, but the roots and crowns are **perennial.**

All brambles send up new shoots or canes from the crown of the plant during each growing season. Red and yellow raspberries develop new shoots from **both** the crown and roots.

These new canes, whether from crown or roots, will grow vigorously during the summer, initiate flower buds in the fall, overwinter and then bear the following season. This fruit is borne on the leafy shoots which arise from lateral (side) buds on the one-year-old canes. Once having borne their crop,

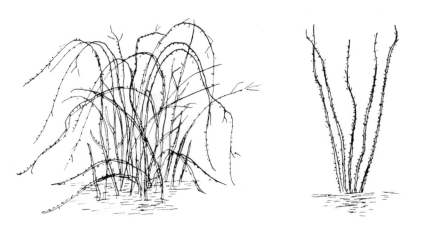

*Raspberry plants left unpruned will become a mass of brambles. Prune for larger fruit and easier care. Unpruned plant at left is shown at right after being properly cut back. Cut canes of Red Raspberries back to about 30 inches.*

the canes start a gradual process of d●ng up and begin to die back shortly after the fruit is harvested. They should be cut and burned. New shoots soon will begin developing to repeat the cycle and provide next year's fruiting canes.

In late March or early April before bud growth starts, trim back last year's growth of canes. These will be the canes that bear this year. Remember, this second season's bearing canes will be neither numerous nor large, for raspberries take three years before there is sufficient growth for a large crop. This first pruning should see the canes cut back a quarter of their growth.

The second pruning takes place *after* the canes bear fruit. As soon as the berries have all been picked, cut the canes which bore fruit (and any others that are broken) close to the ground. Remove and burn them. This will permit the new shoots to have sun and air, and will reduce the possibility of disease spreading from the old canes. Be sure to thin out any weak new canes, giving the ones you decide to keep sufficient growing room.

By the third season, if you have either mulched or cultivated according to directions, you should have fine, husky plants, seven to 10 feet tall. From the third season on you should cut these back in late March or early April about a third of their length. Do this before their bud growth starts.

*After old canes have borne fruit they should be cut off close to the ground, moved elsewhere, and burned. This will help to prevent disease.*

**Pruning Everbearers**

While cutting the canes after they fruit and die back is the approved method for most raspberries, the everbearers have a different life style. They bear fruit twice on the same cane. The new shoots bear a crop at the tips in the fall and bear again the next season further down on the canes.

For this reason the fruit canes of the everbearers should not be pruned after bearing the fall crop, since this would remove the fruiting wood for the spring crop.

For those who prefer one large crop to two smaller ones there is still another way. Everbearing varieties will produce abundant fruit on primocanes (canes of the current season's growth), and thus it is possible to grow them only for the fall crop. This is accomplished by mowing all of the canes to within two or three inches of the ground in the spring, before growth starts. In the fall only the abundant crop on the primocanes is harvested. There are several advantages in doing this: it eliminates all the labor of hand pruning, winter-injured canes present no problems, and fungus diseases are held to a minimum as well.

## Growing Red Raspberries

In training the reds, you either may keep all suckers pulled (which will limit your number of plants to just what you started out with), or you can let some of the suckers grow within the row to form a hedge. For a hedge, set your plants three feet apart; for individual bushes set them four feet apart. For either, if you plant in parallel rows, space the rows five feet apart.

Keep the soil well cultivated for the first few months after planting. Start applying mulch about the middle of the summer after the canes for next year's growth are well up. This will conserve moisture and keep down weeds.

The following spring all of last year's dead canes should be cut out and removed. Head back the new ones to about 30 inches. They will then put out lateral branches which will bear fruit in midsummer. Leave five to eight fruiting canes per hill for mature plants, and at this time also remove any weak canes.

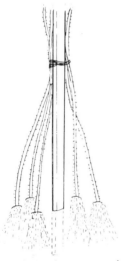

*Red Raspberries may be trained and pruned to the staked hill system. Do not bunch canes up too tightly or they will not have good air circulation.*

Red raspberries properly pruned usually are able to stand well without support, but if they need help here is what to do:

Drive a stake beside each plant and tie the canes loosely to it. Do not bunch them up too tightly or they will not have good air circulation. If you are growing your reds hedgestyle, set posts at the end of each row, stretch a wire between them and tie the canes to the wire.

To keep your raspberries within bounds you will have to control their enthusiasm for producing unwanted suckers. With the hill system, these should be pulled up from the very start. If you want your raspberries to establish themselves as a hedge, let the suckers develop in the row about 10 inches apart. Pull up any that appear at the sides. Once the hedge is established keep all new ones pulled. And when I say "pull up" I mean *exactly* that! Cutting them just makes them grow again even more eagerly.

If red raspberries grow well in your climate you can propagate indefinitely from the first variety you plant. Just dig up healthy suckers and plant them in a new location.

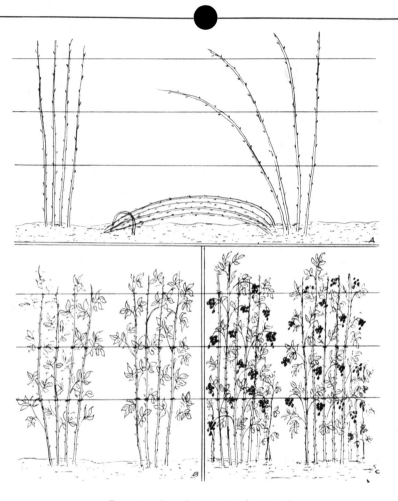

### Growing Raspberries in the North

A. In the fall, after the first killing frost, prune long raspberry canes back to 6 feet. Bend canes down and lay them flat on the ground, parallel to the row, securing them so they will not pull back up again. Dig a trench between rows 1½ feet wide by 8 or 9 inches deep. Mound soil from the trench over the canes. This is well worth the effort where winter temperatures are severe.

B. Straighten canes after uncovering and tie to the supporting wires. Cut them back if they are longer than 6 feet. Allow about four canes to each root.

C. In early summer new canes will start from base of plant. Again choose four healthy sturdy canes and allow them to develop. Try to choose canes about 6 to 8 inches apart. Remove canes, by cutting off at ground, that have borne fruit.

## Growing Black Raspberries

Black raspberries are, if anything, even more eager than the reds to continue propagating themselves. They are constantly arching over their canes and burying the tips in the ground, and every time they do this the tips take root and a new plant grows. If unchecked you will soon have a jungle, so restrain them properly.

Pruning should begin with the blacks as soon as the new shoots are 18 to 20 inches tall. At this height the tops are pinched off to make the canes branch. This makes them sturdier and easier to manage, and if it is not done they become long and sprawling. This operation, called **tipping**, will prevent the bush from growing taller and also keep your plants under control so they cannot form tip plants. And it makes them put out laterals which will bear the following year. By late summer or early fall the laterals will be several feet long, and a number of fruit buds will have developed. During the winter both the canes and the laterals will "sleep" in what is called dormant rest.

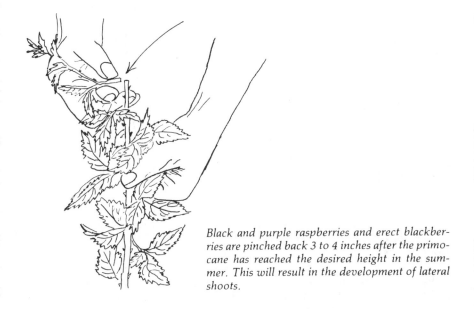

*Black and purple raspberries and erect blackberries are pinched back 3 to 4 inches after the primocane has reached the desired height in the summer. This will result in the development of lateral shoots.*

While blacks should not be planted quite as deeply as the reds, it is good to give them more space—five feet apart within the rows and the rows also five or six feet apart. Cultivate the soil and follow a mulching program just as for the reds.

*13*

In the spring, while the canes are still dormant, the laterals should be cut back to five or six buds. The choice is yours: the more fruit buds you leave the more berries; the fewer the buds the larger the fruit.

Here is something it is well to remember, too. If you want to grow both red and black raspberries you should put a considerable distance between the two types. This is because the reds sometimes carry a disease that does them little or no harm but may prove near fatal to the blacks. (Diseases and Insect Pests—Turn to the following section on Blackberries for full notes on the few disease and insect problems that are encountered in growing raspberries.)

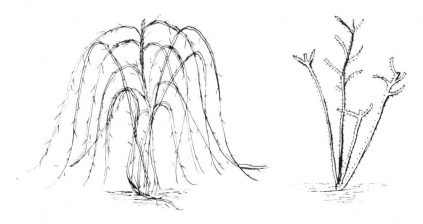

*Left: Black raspberry plant before pruning. Right: Same plant after pruning.*

## Harvesting

Delicious and desirable as it is, the raspberry fruit is also delicate and perishable, so use care in harvesting. Pick the fruit often and when fully ripe. Reds are best when they are a deep garnet and begin to push away from the stem.

I find they are of the best flavor when picked in the late afternoon, and I always pick in small baskets and never press them down. Also I pick only the best, for there is often a surprising difference in the quality of the berries growing on the same plant.

After picking I remove the berries to a cool storage place as soon as possible. If washing is necessary I place them in very cold water (or chill them first in the refrigerator), and wash quickly, draining them on paper towels. I like to serve them well chilled, and in a shallow dish, so they will not be crushed. And they look very attractive in a large saucer or a shallow bowl so they can be seen and admired. This is a fruit that is also fun to "eat with your eyes."

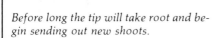

To root black raspberries throw a bit of
earth over the tip, letting a few leaves
extend upright and weight with a brick
or stone.

*Before long the tip will take root and be-*
*gin sending out new shoots.*

Let these grow until the following
spring. When plants are well formed, cut
back parent cane. Transplant new plant,
if desired, to another location.

## Freezing Raspberries

Raspberries are easy to freeze and will give you delicious desserts all
through the year. Make a sugar pack by mixing ¾ cup of sugar with each
quart (1-⅓ lb.) of berries, or use a 40 percent syrup (3 cups of sugar dis-
solved in 4 cups of water).

Select only firm, fully ripe berries of ight color and good quality. Wash in iced water, sort and drain thoroughly. Cover berries with cold syrup, package, seal and freeze.

If you have the space you can freeze berries in a shallow layer on a cookie sheet, sift sugar over them when frozen and package in bags. I use these to top ice cream and other desserts.

And speaking of desserts, have you ever tried Red Raspberry Swirls?

### Red Raspberry Swirls

| | |
|---|---|
| Red raspberries, frozen . . . . . . . . . . . | About 10 ounces |
| Flour, unsifted . . . . . . . . . . . . . . . . . | 1 cup |
| Baking powder . . . . . . . . . . . . . . . . . | 1½ teaspoons |
| Sugar . . . . . . . . . . . . . . . . . . . . . . . . | 1½ teaspoons |
| Salt . . . . . . . . . . . . . . . . . . . . . . . . . | ¼ teaspoon |
| Shortening . . . . . . . . . . . . . . . . . . . . | 3 tablespoons |
| Milk . . . . . . . . . . . . . . . . . . . . . . . . . | 6 tablespoons |
| Butter or margarine, melted . . . . . . . | 1 tablespoon |
| Sugar . . . . . . . . . . . . . . . . . . . . . . . . | 1 tablespoon |
| Quick-cooking tapioca . . . . . . . . . . . | 1½ teaspoons |

Thaw and drain raspberries, saving the juice. Mix flour, baking powder, 1½ teaspoons sugar and salt thoroughly. Cut in shortening with pastry blender or fork until well mixed. Stir in milk slowly, using just enough to make a dough that is soft but not sticky.

Preheat oven to 425°F. (hot). Turn dough onto lightly floured surface and roll into 8- by 12-inch rectangle. Brush dough with melted fat, spread berries over it, and sprinkle with 1 tablespoon sugar.

Roll as for jelly roll, starting at the 12-inch side. Cut into six 2-inch slices. Combine raspberry juice and tapioca; heat to a boil. Cook 2 minutes, stirring often. Pour into 7- by 7- by 2-inch baking pan. Place dough slices in hot juice mixture. Bake 25 to 30 minutes or until browned.

## Medicinal Qualities of Raspberries

Raspberries are a good source of Vitamin C and are considered a good blood and skin cleanser. They are reputed to be helpful in cases of high blood pressure, obesity, congested liver, constipation and menstrual cramps. The foliage of the raspberry shrub possesses a very active principal called **fragrine.** Tea made from the raspberry leaves is used as a remedy for diarrhea—you drink it cold.

To make tea place one ounce of leaves in one-and-one-half pints of water and simmer for 20 minutes. You may sweeten with a little honey. It is said that this warm tea also tends to produce normal menstrual flow and, if taken during pregnancy, will help make childbirth easier.

# Growing Better Blackberries

There's no doubt about it. While raspberries with care can be easily grown in the South, they will do much better in the North and East. Blackberries, on the other hand, are a pushover for those who live in a more temperate climate. Yet, by careful choice of variety they can also be grown in colder regions.

Check the "Hardiness Chart" at the end of this bulletin to find the variety that will do best in your zone. Note that **Alfred,** given winter protection, will even grow in Zone 4. Also the fine new variety, **Darrow,** originated at the New York Experiment Station is noteworthy among blackberries for its vigor, reliably heavy production, firmness and good quality. The plants appeared hardier than all other selections and varieties in the Station planting. Berries are one inch long, ¾ inch wide, long, conic, and are glossy black. They begin ripening early (or about the same as **Eldorado)** and continue over a long period. **Darrow** also does well for me in Southern Oklahoma and I prefer it to all other varieties.

Actually there are two types of blackberries—erect and trailing—and they differ primarily in the character of their canes. Erect blackberries have arched, self-supporting canes. The trailing blackberries (also called dewberries, ground blackberries, or running blackberries) have canes that are not self-supporting and must be tied to poles or trellises in cultivation.

The two types also differ in fruit characteristics. Fruit clusters of the trailing blackberry are more open than those of the erect blackberry. Trailing blackberries generally ripen earlier and are often larger and sweeter than the erect type.

## Choosing a Planting Site

Always consider the availability of soil moisture, for this is the most important factor in choosing a planting site for blackberries. As the fruit grows and ripens, it will need a large supply of moisture. During the winter, however, the plants are harmed if water stands around their roots, so drainage is also important.

Almost any soil type, except very sandy soils, is suitable for blackberries as long as the drainage is good. The exact pH preference is between 5.0 and 6.0, but this can be slanted a little either way.

In areas where winters are severe, the slope of the planting site is important. Blackberries planted on hillsides are in less danger of winter injury and damage from late spring frosts than those planted in valleys. In sections where drying winds occur frequently, the plantation should be sheltered by surrounding hills, trees or shrubs.

## Planting

Blackberries should be planted as soon as you can prepare the soil—in early spring in the North, in late winter or early spring in the South.

### Preparing the Soil

Prepare the soil for blackberries just as thoroughly as you would for a garden. For best results, plow to a depth of about nine inches as soon as the soil is in a workable condition. Just before setting the plants the soil should be disked and harrowed. This, of course, applies to the larger planting. For a home garden go over the area with a rotary tiller.

Just as with raspberries, it is a good idea to seed and plow under one or two green-manure crops before establishing a new blackberry planting. This may be rye, vetch or cowpeas. This thorough working gets the soil in good condition for planting, and the added organic matter and nitrogen help the plantation to produce an early fruit crop.

As with raspberries, you can take a soil sample of the area to be planted and make any corrections needed beforehand. The pH preference of blackberries is between 5.0 and 6.0—much the same as for raspberries. They do well in ordinary soil, thriving best in clay loam that is moist yet well drained.

### Spacing the Plants

Plant erect varieties of blackberries five feet apart in rows that are eight feet apart. Space vigorous varieties of trailing or semitrailing blackberries, such as **Thornless Evergreen,** eight to 12 feet apart in rows 10 feet apart. Space other trailing varieties four to six feet apart in rows eight feet apart.

In the central states, set erect varieties two feet apart in rows nine to 10 feet apart, and let the plants grow into hedgerows.

## Setting the Plants

When setting out my plants I am always careful not to let the planting stock dry out. If I cannot plant the stock as soon as it arrives, I protect the roots from drying by heeling in the plants.

To heel in, I dig a trench deep enough to contain the roots. Then I spread the plants along the trench, roots down, and cover the roots with moist soil.

If the plants are dry when I receive them, I soak the roots in water for several hours before planting or heeling them in.

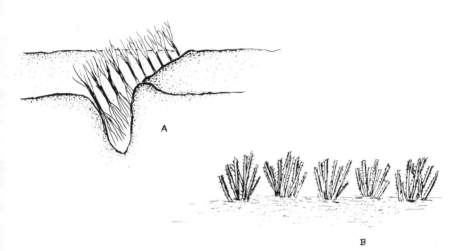

*When your stock arrives open and examine it as soon as possible. If you cannot plant at once, store it for a few days by covering the roots with some type of moist material and store in a cool place, away from wind and sun so it will not dry.*

*If you must hold it more than 2 or 3 days it should be heeled in. Dig a trench (A) and bury the roots in the ground. (B) Pack soil firmly around the roots to prevent air pockets and keep the soil moist until ready to plant.*

*Be sure to plant in permanent location before buds begin to swell.*

When I am ready to set the plants in their permanent location I dip the roots in a thin mud made with clay and water (or I keep the plants in polyethylene bags). This coating helps to protect the roots from rapid drying while the plants are being set.

Before setting the plants, I cut the tops back so they are about six inches long. The six-inch top is useful as a handle when setting the plants and will serve to show their location.

I find the best way to make a planting is to cut a slit in the soil with the blade of a mattock or shovel, pressing the handle of the tool forward to open the slit. Then I put the root of the blackberry plant in the hole, setting it so it

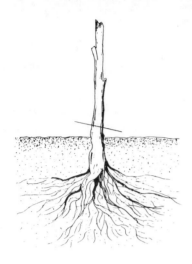

*Proper planting depth for strong, well-rooted Blackberry.*

is about the same depth as it was in the nursery. Then I withdraw the blade of the mattock or shovel and pack the soil firmly around the root with my heel.

### Intercropping

During the first summer after the blackberry plants have been set, I find it possible to grow vegetables between the rows. Such vegetables as cabbage, cauliflower, beans, peas and summer squash are good for intercropping. Do not, however, try to grow grain crops, since they are not cultivated and they take too much moisture and nutrients needed by the blackberry plants.

## Training Plants the Way They Should Go

Blackberry plants are best trained to trellises. While erect types can be grown without support, many of the canes may be broken during cultivation and picking. Trellises will pay for themselves by reducing this damage.

While many trellis arrangements and methods of training are used by blackberry growers, I believe the simplest method of trellis construction and training is as follows:

Build trellises by stretching wire between posts set 15 to 20 feet apart in the row. For erect blackberries, use a single wire attached to the posts about 30 inches from the ground. For semi-trailing and trailing blackberries it is best to use two wires, one about three feet and the other about five feet from the ground.

I like to tie the canes to the wires with soft string. Erect varieties are best tied where the canes cross the wire. Then tie trailing canes horizontally along the wires or fan them out from the ground and tie them where they cross each wire. Because the canes need air circulation around them they never should be tied in bundles.

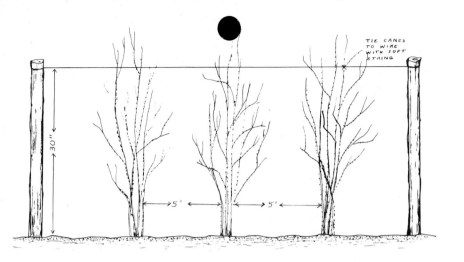

*Trellis for Blackberries*
Erect Blackberry plants can be grown without support but many of the canes may be broken during cultivation and picking. Trellises will often pay for themselves by reducing this damage.

A simple trellis may be made by stretching wire between posts set 15 to 20 feet apart in the row. Use a single wire attached to the post about 30 inches from the ground.

Tie the canes to the wires with soft string where the canes cross the wire. Avoid tying the canes in bundles.

## To Prune and Thin

The crowns of blackberry plants are *perennial*, new canes arising from them each year. These canes are *biennial*—that is they live for only two years, and during the first year they grow and send out laterals (side branches). Small branches grow from buds on the laterals in the second year, and the fruit is borne on these buds. After the laterals bear fruit, the canes die.

Be sure to prune the laterals back in the spring, so the fruit will be larger and of better quality (than fruit from unpruned laterals). Pruning is best done before growth starts, and the laterals should be cut back to a length of about 12 inches.

Growing blackberries is almost too easy, especially with the erect types which send up root suckers in addition to the new canes (that arise from the crown). Don't let all these root suckers grow, or your blackberry planting will soon turn into a thicket.

Take care during the growing season to remove all suckers that appear between the rows. And you must pull the suckers out of the ground. Those that are pulled will not regrow as ⬤ly as those that are cut down.

Cut off the tips of erect blackberry canes when they reach a height of 30 to 36 inches. This will make the canes branch. Also tipped canes are much sturdier and are better able to support a heavy fruit crop than untipped ones.

In summer, just as soon as the last berries have been harvested, it is wise to cut out all the old canes and burn them. At this time I like to thin out the new canes as well, leaving three or four canes of erect varieties, four to eight canes of semi-trailing varieties, and eight to 12 canes of trailing varieties.

If you live in an area where anthracnose and rosette are serious diseases problems for blackberries, cut out *all* the canes—both old and new—after fruiting. Then fertilize and cultivate to promote growth of replacement canes for the next year's crop. These two diseases seldom are troublesome except in some areas of the South.

If suckers are allowed to form within the rows of erect blackberries, thin them to about five or six per lineal foot of row.

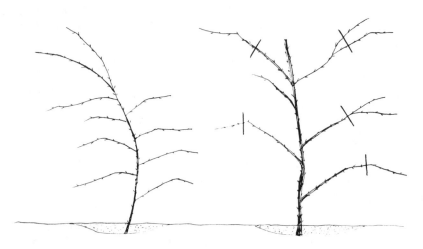

*Blackberry*
*Pruning makes the difference. Note sturdy plant on the right. This plant was pruned during the summer and will be pruned the following spring where the black marks indicate.*

## Fertilizing

In a large planting, barley, oats or buckwheat make excellent cover crops for blackberries because they do not live over the winter. They should be worked into the soil in autumn and additional humus added if possible. These crops also help in giving winter protection to berry canes. For the smaller home planting, compost or well-decomposed manure are helpful. It is believed now by most authorities that chemical fertilizers such as the nitrates increase cane growth, but not the formation of more fruit.

Some varieties of blackberry are self-sterile and need a pollenizer. Two varieties in the garden, which blossom at the same time so that the blossoms may be crossed, often give better fruit results.

Blackberries, as I said earlier, need a moist soil during the fruiting season, and poor quality berries often result on dry soil. The moist condition in the soil can best be assured by the use of abundant compost.

## Cultivating

Blackberry plantings should be cultivated thoroughly and frequently. Don't let grass and weeds get a start and become difficult to control. Begin cultivating in the spring very early, just as soon as the soil is workable. Cultivate throughout the season as often as necessary to keep weeds down. As often as once a week, if you must. Discontinue cultivation at least a month before freezing weather normally begins.

To avoid harming shallow roots of the plants, cultivate only two or three inches deep near the rows. For a large planting, a tractor-mounted grape hoe or a rotary hoe may be used for cultivating in the rows and under trellises. A tiller works best for home plantings.

Winter cover crops help prevent soil erosion, add humus to the soil and also shield the canes during the winter from drying winds. It is a good idea to sow a cover crop at the time of the last cultivation. In addition to those already mentioned, such crops as cowpeas, spring oats or rye may be used, drilled in the middles and leaving 12 to 15 inches next to the plants free of cover crop. Plant a cover crop best suited to your area and winter conditions. Then turn it under the following spring.

## Propagating Blackberries

Blackberries are easy to propagate, the erect plants from root suckers or root cuttings, the latter method yielding the greatest number of new plants. Trailing blackberries and some semi-trailing varieties are propagated by burying the tips of the canes, which will root and form new plants.

*Erect blackberry plants are easily propagated by root suckers or root cuttings. Root cuttings will yield the greatest number of new plants. These new plants should be pruned as indicated in the drawing.*

## "Trailing Blackberries"

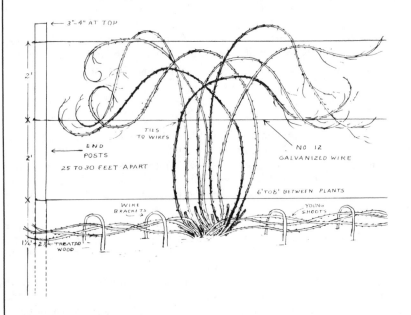

Method of training Dewberries, Boysenberries and Youngberries, sometimes called "trailing Blackberries." All three of these berries tend to grow in a rather sprawling manner—like lazy teenagers—and the fruiting canes will need support, otherwise the berries will get very dirty. They will also form unwanted tip plants if allowed to bend down.

Young shoots of the present year's growth are kept on the ground and fastened with wire brackets to keep them out of the way. Fruiting canes are looped over trellis and cut off close to the ground after bearing.

In the Northern states the canes kept on the ground may be covered with earth and mulch during the winter months. In the spring divide the canes from one hill about equally and wrap them around the wires running each direction from the plant.

## To Foil the Birds

Birds are sometimes troublesome in and around the blackberry patch. If you find this to be true, try luring them away by planting mulberries, elderberries or chokecherries which they often prefer. With these fruits to attract them they will leave the blackberries alone.

# Harvesting

Pick your blackberries as soon as they become sweet. Be *sure* they are fully ripe, for the fruit is not ready for picking when it first turns black. You may need to do a little testing and tasting. Berries that are picked at the proper time, handled carefully and stored in a cool place will stay in good condition for several days. Berries that are over-ripe or injured spoil quickly.

The fruit should be fully ripened but firm. Pick often—for most varieties every other day. Pick early in the day and try to finish before the hottest part of the day. Blackberries do not spoil as quickly if picked in the morning as when picked in the afternoon. Do not crush or bruise the fruit—place it carefully in the baskets—and as soon as each basket is full, place it in a basket carrier, which should always be kept in the shade.

# Freezing Berries

Berries are easy to freeze and will give you delicious desserts all through the year. Make a sugar syrup by dissolving 3 cups of sugar in 4 cups of water. Stir to dissolve but do not heat. Or use a sugar pack, mixing ¾ cup of sugar with each quart of berries (1-⅓ lb.).

Select only firm, fully ripe berries of bright color. Wash in iced water, sort and drain thoroughly. Cover berries with cold syrup, package, seal and freeze.

Blackberries are wonderful for many things, including wines and jellies, but when I think "blackberry" I also think "cobbler." Here is a really great recipe:

## Blackberry Cobbler

| | |
|---|---|
| 1 egg | 2 teaspons baking powder |
| 1 cup sugar | ½ teaspoon salt |
| 3 tablespoons margarine, melted | 4 cups firm, ripe blackberries |
| ⅓ cup milk | ¼ teaspoon ground nutmeg |
| 1½ cups sifted, all purpose flour | ¼ teaspoon ground cinnamon |

Beat together egg, ½ cup sugar, the margarine and milk. Sift together flour, baking powder and salt. Beat into egg mixture. Combine blackberries, remaining sugar, nutmeg and cinnamon. Put in oiled baking dish (12 × 8 × 2 inches). Top fruit with batter, spreading smoothly. Bake in pre-heated, moderate oven (375°F.) for 30 minutes, or until crust is crisp and golden brown. Serve hot with cream, custard or hard sauce.

# Nutritional and Medicinal Properties

Blackberries contain vitamins A and C and are said to be useful to cool the blood, as a nerve tonic, a laxative, an aid for anaemia general debility, for gastric weaknesses and skin problems. Pulped blackberry leaves sometimes are applied to burns and foot blisters. Leaves intended for tea should be collected young and tender and are good combined with three parts each of wild strawberry and woodruff leaves and a pinch of thyme. Chop the leaves, pour boiling water over them, steep for three to five minutes and sweeten with honey. This tea is thirst-quenching and diuretic. There seems to be complete agreement among all authorities on the value of any form of blackberry extraction, whether from root, bark, berry or leaf. No household should be without one or another form of such a simple remedy for unexpected intestinal upsets.

### Blackberry Cordial

For many people a safe and convenient form of remedial blackberry is in the form of blackberry brandy or cordial. This is easily made with the juice of fresh berries, sugar and a few spices boiled together, with brandy added.

Another recipe for preparing an astringent potion from the dried root-bark of blackberries calls for an ounce of the root to be boiled down in 1½ pints of milk or water to a pint. Drinking half a cupful every hour or two is said to be helpful in cases of diarrhea, but if you use the fresh root, a larger dose is required. Dried blackberry root-bark contains tannin, gallic acid and villosin. To a lesser extent the juice of the fresh fruit also contains these properties.

# Diseases and Insects of Raspberries and Blackberries

I will not go into insects and diseases in great detail because if you follow the directions given for soil preparation and management you will not be troubled greatly with either. However, a few points should be emphasized:

• Be sure to buy your stock from a reliable, registered grower who has disease-free plants.

• As soon as old canes have completed bearing, be sure to remove them from the patch and burn them if possible.

• When pruning, never crowd canes. Leave plenty of room for good air circulation and sunlight.

## Diseases

**Anthracnose,** a foliage disease most severe in the Southeast, can be controlled by sanitation and by spraying with liquid lime sulfur (1 part per 9 parts water) in the spring when the new leaves are unfolded ½ to ¾ of an inch.

**Leaf and cane spot** is a fungus disease common in the Southeast and the Pacific Northwest. Purple spots with white centers develop on leaves and canes, sometimes causing early defoliation and weakening the canes. Cut out and remove the infected canes from the field after harvest. Spraying with lime sulfur (as recommended for anthracnose) also will help in control.

**Double blossom,** a fungus disease infecting blackberry plants in the Southeast, causes flowerbuds to enlarge and produce coarse, reddish flowers with twisted petals which make the flowers appear double. These flowers will not produce fruit, and the infected plants also develop abnormal broomlike growth of leafy shoots. To control the disease, cut *all* the canes close to the ground after harvest and remove them.

**Fruit rots,** caused by several fungi, ● infect the fruit of bramble berries before or after harvest. The infected fruit is usually overgrown with a gray or black cottony fungus mass. The fruit rot fungi are universally present, but develop most readily on damaged and over-ripe berries. To control the disease, carefully pick the sound fruit at frequent intervals and quickly store the fruit under refrigeration at 32° to 40°F.

**Sterility,** a virus disease that causes blackberry plants to produce completely or partially sterile flowers, is common in the East. The infected plants grow vigorously without apparent symptoms until fruiting time. To control sterility, use only plant stocks that are free from this virus, and eliminate unfruitful plants whenever they are found.

## Insects

Raspberries and blackberries are comparatively free from insect injury, but the fruit or foliage may become infested with aphids, leafhoppers, mites, sawflies, scales, fruitworms, stinkbugs, leaf rollers, beetles and weevils.

Also watch for cane borers, whose work on both raspberries and blackberries usually becomes apparent about in July. There is no known remedy, so when you see signs of damage, cut the cane below the infested portion and burn the part removed. You can recognize the damage by examining all wilted or broken canes and locating tiny holes made by this small, white grub. If you don't get the borer it will work its way down into the crown of the root and destroy the entire plant.

If Japanese beetles are present in your locality they will be attracted to raspberries. Ask your County Agricultural Agent the best means of control, or try Milky Spore Disease, now obtainable from many nurseries and garden centers.

Damage from most other insects can be kept at a minimum if these general suggestions are followed:

- Prune out insect-infested canes and burn them.
- Remove old canes after harvest.

Where there are severe infestations and damage, however, malathion (a comparatively safe insecticide), may be used for aphids, Japanese beetles, rose leaf hoppers or rose scale. Lime sulfur may be used (on dormant plants only) for red mites. Rotenone may be applied for raspberry fruit worms on the foliage when the buds appear but before they open. It also may be applied on the foliage just before the plants bloom (and be repeated in about two weeks) to control the red-necked cane borer.

I do not like to use pesticides on berry plants as I consider them self-defeating. There are "good" insects, as well as "bad," and the honey bee is a primary pollinator. Many are killed, particularly if a pesticide is used when the plants are in blossom. Honey bees are of great value, especially in a planting of self-unfruitful blackberries which require cross-pollination.

If a variety of blackberry in a large planting is known to require cross-pollination, you should insure a sufficient supply of pollinators. Place a colony of honey bees in or near the field.

Raspberry Fruitworm

Rose Chafer

Aphid

Grasshopper

Snail

Red Spider

Japanese Beetle

Borer (Larvae)

Cutworm

*Insects Injurious to Small Fruits and Berries*

Aphid:      *Adult and young, very tiny. Green to greenish-brown. Soft bodied. Covered with a fine, whitish wax. Aphids cluster on leaves.*

Damage:   *Curled and distorted leaves.*

Control:   *Dust or spray with malathion.*

Cutworm: *Many species. Cutworms are dull gray, brown or black and may be striped or spotted. They are stout, soft bodied and smooth, and up to 1¼ inches long. They curl up tightly when disturbed.*

Damage:   *Cut off plants, at or below soil surface. Some cutworms feed on leaves, buds or fruits; others feed on the underground portions of plants.*

Control:   *You can prevent cutworm injury to many plants without using an insecticide by placing a stiff 3-inch cardboard collar around the stems; allow this to extend about 1 inch into the soil and protrude 2 inches above the soil. If used for Strawberries clear the stem by about ½ inch.*

Snail: Snails, gray or black in col⬤ve rounded shells. They and a related species called, Slugs (which ⬤e no shells) are often a great nuisance, especially in very wet seasons.

Control: Putting salt on the soft bodied species dissolves them. Both snails and slugs can be trapped in beer cans or in receptacles containing a small amount of beer.

Japanese Beetles: Adult: Shiny metallic green; oval; coppery-brown outer wings; about ½ inch long and ¼ inch wide.

 Larva: White body; brown head, up to 1 inch long when fully grown.

Damage: Adults may attack foliage of Raspberry, Blackberry etc.

Control: Dust or spray with malathion. Or obtain Milky Spore Disease which is sold by nurseries or garden centers for control of Japanese Beetle Grubs.

Red Necked Cane Borer: Adult: Dark-bronze or black beetle, shiny, copper-red neck, slender, about 1 inch long.

 Larva: White; flat head, slender; up to ¾ inch long.

Damage: Adults eat margins of leaves; larvae tunnel canes, causing spindle-shaped swellings on surfaces.

Control: Cut off infested canes well below the points of injury and destroy them.

Raspberry Fruitworm—Several species. Adults:  Yellow to brown beetles; ¼ inch long.

 Larvae:  Brown and white; up to ⅛ inch long.

Damage: Adults make long, narrow slits in blossom buds and newly formed leaves; larvae feed in berries.

Control: Rotonone dust or spray is effective when applied 3 times at 10-day intervals  starting  7 days after the first blossoms appear.

Rose Chafer: Gray or fawn-colored beetle; reddish-brown head; long-legged and slender; ½ inch long. If not present in large numbers, remove by hand.

Damage: Feeds on foliage, buds, flowers and fruits of Blackberry, and Raspberry.

Red Spider: Several species. Adults and young: Tiny (barely visible to the naked eye); red or greenish red. Found on undersides of leaves. Not classified as insects.

Damage: Yellow specks and fine webs on leaves; plants and fruits are stunted. Attack Blackberry and other small fruits.

Control: Malathion. Partial control may be obtained by applying a dust containing 25 to 30 percent of sulfur or by applying a spray containing sulfur.

Grasshopper: Many species. Adults and nymphs. Brown, gray, black or yellow; strong hind legs, up to 2 inches long. Most grasshoppers are strong flyers.

Damage: When present in great numbers will destroy leaves of berry plants.

Control: Apply a dust or spray containing malathion.

**Choose Disease-resistant Varieties Such as These:**

BLACKBERRIES: **Darrow, Eldorad⬤ ⬤lfred**
BLACK RASPBERRIES: **Morrison, New Logan, Cumberland, Black Hawk**
RED RASPBERRIES: **Virus-free Latham, Virus-free Newburg, Boyne, Gatineau Red, Sunrise**
EVERBEARING RED RASPBERRIES: **Fall Red, Regent, Indian Summer, Heritage. (Indan Summer** is superior to Regent.) **Fall Red,** introduced by the University of New Hampshire, is super-hardy.

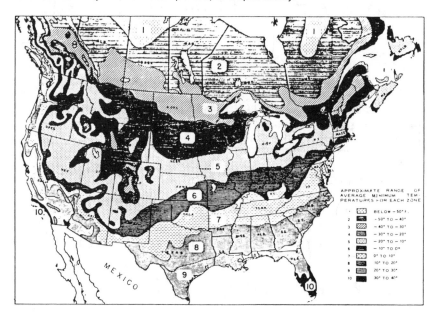

## HARDINESS OF BLACKBERRY VARIETIES BY TEMPERATURE ZONES

| Variety | Zone | Variety | Zone |
|---|---|---|---|
| Alfred | 4,* 5, 6 | Georgia Thornless | 9 |
| Aurora [b] | 8 | Hedrick | 5,* 6, 7 [c] |
| Austin Thornless | 7,* 8 | Hillquist | 6,* 7, 8 [c] |
| Bailey | 5, 6 | Himalaya | 7, 8 |
| Boysen | 7, 8 | Jerseyblack | 6, 7 |
| Brainerd | 6,* 7, 8 | Lawton | 6,* 7, 8 [c] |
| Brazos | 8, 9 | Logan | 7,* 8 [c] |
| Cascade [b] | 7,* 8 [c] | Lucretia | 7, 8 [c] |
| Chehalem [b] | 7,* 8 [c] | Mammoth [b] | 7,* 8 [c] |
| Cory Thornless [b] | 7,* 8 | Marion [b] | 8 [c] |
| Dallas | 6,* 7, 8 [c] | Mayes | 7,* 8 |
| Darrow | 5, 6, 7 | Midnite | 6,* 7, 8 [c] |
| Dewblack | 6,* 7, 8 [c] | Nanticoke | 6, 7, 8 |
| Early Harvest | 6,* 7, 8 [c] | Oklawaha | 9 |
| Early Wonder | 6,* 7, 8 | Olallie [b] | 8 [c] |
| Ebony King | 5,* 6, 7 | Ranger | 6,* 7 |
| Eldorado | 5, 6, 7 | Raven | 6,* 7 |
| Erie | 5, 6, 7 [c] | Smoothstem | 7, 8 [c] |
| Evergreen [b] | 8 [c] | Snyder | 5, 6 |
| Flint | 7, 8 | Thornfree | 6,* 7, 8 [c] |
| Flordagrand | 9 | Williams | 8 |
| Gem | 8 | Young | 6,* 7, 8 |

* Subject to winter injury in some years if not protected.
[b] Not adapted to States east of Arizona.
[c] Adapted to northern part of zone or higher elevations.

# Raspberries

Prune at top after fall fruiting.
Prune at bottom after spring fruiting.
10-10-10 fertilizer. (Do not over fertilize)
Cease fertilization after June.
Water during morning hours.

# Blackberries

Prune laterals down to 12" in spring.

Cut off tips of blackberry canes when reach a height of 30" to 36."

In summer soon as berries have been harvested, Cut out old canes. Thin out new canes:

Erect - leave 3 or 4 canes
Semi trailing - 4 to 8 canes
Trailing - 8 - 12 canes

Pull out suckers between rows.